CYNTHIA RYLANT

The Journey

Stories of Migration

illustrated by

LAMBERT DAVIS

THE BLUE SKY PRESS
An Imprint of Scholastic Inc. · New York

Introduction

MOST creatures live out their lives in the places where they are born. The tiny mouse runs in the fields where his mother ran. The gray squirrel lives in the same tall trees all her life. The cow stays on the farm.

But there are some creatures who do not stay where they are born, who cannot stay. These are the creatures who migrate. Their lives will be spent moving from one place to another. Some will migrate to survive. Some will migrate to create new life. All will be remarkable.

Here are the stories of some of these remarkable travelers. The locust, the whale, the eel, the butterfly, the caribou, the tern — so different from each other but so alike in one profound way: Each must *move*.

The Locusts

THERE ARE few migrations as dramatic and frightening as when the desert locusts are moving across Africa. These insects are actually young grasshoppers, and grasshoppers usually do not travel.

But sometimes too many grasshopper eggs are laid in one small area, and when the grasshoppers are born, there isn't enough food. The grasshoppers now have only one choice for survival: to migrate in search of vegetation.

And so these grasshoppers will begin changing. Their bodies will turn from light green to dark yellow or red. Their antennae will grow short rather than long. And when they rise up to fly together by the *billions*, they will be grasshoppers no more. They will be locusts.

A cloud of desert locusts in the sky is an unbelievable sight. There are so many locusts that they block out the sun. It seems like night. And in the sudden darkness there is a terrible thunderous noise. It is the noise of a billion wings.

What happens next is even more incredible. When the locusts fly to the ground, they will eat every plant, every blade of grass, every leaf and bush and piece of vegetation as far as the eye can see. Within minutes they will fly off again, leaving behind them a totally devastated landscape.

And though locusts do not willfully hurt people—they want only to eat gardens, trees, bushes, grass—people may die because of the locusts. Because the gardens are empty of food, people may die of starvation.

Desert locusts can also cause accidents. Locusts fly very high—as high as two miles up in the sky—and this can make difficult flying for planes that have to move through the locust cloud. The swarms can also interfere with trains. And millions of crushed locusts on a highway will make cars slip and slide.

There are many stories in history about the terrible devastation of locust plagues. It is written that in ancient times, one locust swarm covered 2,000 square miles.

The swarms today are not nearly as large as that. But they can still be quite big, often as much as one hundred square miles. Imagine so many insects in the sky!

As the locusts migrate in search of food, they ride the winds from one area of rainfall to the next. (There is always more food where it rains.) They travel on sunny mornings and stop in late afternoon to roost for the night.

When they reach a rainy area, they mate and die. Then their eggs will hatch and a new swarm of locusts begins moving. This will happen again and again until one day a swarm will return to the same place where the very first locusts began.

And if the eggs laid are not too many, and if there is plenty of food when the new eggs hatch, there will be no locust swarms for a while. Only pale green grasshoppers moving quietly about.

But someday too many eggs may be laid, and the newly hatched grasshoppers will be much too hungry. These grasshoppers will begin to look a little different and act a little different.

Then they will rise up together by the billions—as desert locusts—and they will fly.

The Whales

MANY MAMMALS migrate, but no mammal migrates as far as the big gray whale. It travels 6,000 miles, then back again—and most of its traveling is done on an empty stomach!

Gray whales love the cold waters near the North Pole because the waters are full of the food they love to eat. The whales live on tiny ocean shrimp and worms, and the Arctic waters are full of these in summer. The whales eat and eat and eat, straining the tiny food through strips of baleen in their mouths. (Instead of teeth, the grays have baleen—long strips of a hard material similar to fingernails.)

The gray whales swim and eat mostly alone through the summer. But in the fall, they will begin to look for some traveling companions, because the whales know one thing for certain:

that they must migrate. In winter, the Arctic seas are going to be filled with solid ice. And the whales will die if they stay.

The first gray whales to leave the Arctic are the pregnant females. These expectant mothers want to have plenty of time to reach the warm waters of California and Mexico before they give birth. No mother wants to have a baby in icy water!

The other whales will follow, and in small groups they will all travel down the Pacific coast. Once they leave the Arctic, the whales won't find much food again, and it may be as long as *eight months* before they eat.

But the whales have stored a lot of fat in their bodies, called blubber, and this will keep them alive.

As they travel, the whales often swim near shore, and people along the way are thrilled. They wave to the whales from rocky cliffs and travel out in boats to say hello to them.

When finally the gray whales reach the warm tropical waters in January, the pregnant females will give birth. And the other whales will mate.

With new calves among them, all of the whales will enjoy life in the peaceful lagoons for a while. Then in March, they will be ready to head back to the Arctic for the summer. They haven't forgotten how they love to eat there!

This time the males will leave first, and the females and calves will stay behind for another several weeks. The calves will have more time to grow and get stronger for the long journey.

Finally, all of the whales will travel, up past Oregon, past Washington, through the waters of Alaska and Asia, up near the North Pole. How do the whales find these Arctic waters? No one is sure. The whales might follow the shape of the ocean beds. They might sense the earth's magnetic field, like living compasses. They may use echolocation—sending out sounds which bounce back and describe what is all around.

But somehow the whales will travel that long 6,000-mile journey north, and they will find the same chilly waters they left behind. When they arrive in the Arctic, they will separate and enjoy a summer of fine ocean eating.

But just before the Arctic winter arrives, before the ice, something will tell the whales to find each other again. To find some company for another long, long swim.

The Eels

MOST FISH are either freshwater fish—these live in lakes and rivers and ponds—or saltwater fish—these live in oceans. Most saltwater fish will die in fresh water. And most freshwater fish would die in the salty ocean.

But there is one amazing fish who somehow survives in both kinds of water. And how it moves from salt water to fresh water—and why—is a fascinating story.

A person seeing an eel swimming in an American river would probably never guess that this fish began its life thousands of miles away, out in the vast Atlantic Ocean, in a mysterious place called the Sargasso Sea.

The Sargasso Sea is mysterious because of its seaweed. Gigantic gardens of thick, wavy seaweed float in the crystal blue water of

the Sargasso Sea, and the strange eeriness of this seaweed has
for centuries inspired stories of monsters living in its darkness.

But monsters don't live in the seaweed of the Sargasso Sea.
Only small ocean creatures swim there. Still, there are some rather
unexpected visitors now and then: They are American silver eels, and
they have come all the way from the freshwater rivers of America
to the salty Sargasso Sea for one singular purpose: to create life.

But these eels probably do not feel like visitors here. For the
Sargasso Sea is where these American eels were born.

Many years ago, these silver eels were very tiny eggs, floating gently in the deep seaweed of the Sargasso Sea.

Then they hatched into larvae. They were only a quarter of an inch long, and they looked like tiny clear leaves.

And where these larvae went next, and how, is remarkable.

The little larvae floated out of the Sargasso Sea and through the vast Atlantic Ocean in only one direction: straight toward America's East Coast. Somehow they actually floated the right way!

For a year these tiny creatures traveled with the ocean's currents.

Who would have known, seeing them, that there was a purpose to their drifting, that one day they would be long, thick eels living in American rivers?

Many of the larvae were eaten by fish, but some were not, and these reached America's Atlantic coast.

Here the larvae grew and changed and looked more like tiny eels than like leaves. Now they were called glass eels because their bodies were so transparent.

The glass eels swam along the coast for a few months, and then they changed again. They grew and became darker and were now yellow eels.

And it was as yellow eels that these small fish began to do something incredible. At least, the females did. For while the males stayed in the salty water along the coast, the female eels turned and swam inland. They left the salt water they had lived in for more than a year, and they went in search of fresh water, in search of the rivers and lakes inside America.

These females were very strong, very determined to find the American rivers where they wanted to live. Some even climbed waterfalls to get there!

The females became freshwater fish. They continued to grow for nearly ten years until they were adults. Now they were about four feet long and were called silver eels. The male eels, still living along the coast, were smaller, only one or two feet long.

And with adulthood, with the urge to mate and continue the pattern of life, the females in the rivers and the males in the ocean knew where they all must go. Ten years or more had passed, but something in them remembered: They remembered the Sargasso Sea.

So the female eels living inside America somehow found their way back to the Atlantic Ocean. They traveled up rivers and even, when necessary, crossed over land, wriggling their fish bodies through the wet grass. The eels survived in the grass because their thick skin did not dry out as quickly as ordinary fish skin.

The females and males all swam away from America, out into the vast Atlantic. Incredibly, again they traveled in exactly

the right direction, back to the Sargasso Sea. How could they possibly find it? Perhaps they sensed particular smells. Perhaps they rode certain ocean currents or felt electrical impulses in the water. Scientists are not sure how the eels navigate.

But as most migrating animals miraculously do, the American silver eels did find the dark seaweed of the wide Sargasso Sea. And here, where their lives began, they mated and died.

In a few weeks, there were new little larvae floating in the Sargasso Sea. They looked like miniature leaves. And though they seemed to have no direction, these creatures knew exactly where they were going.

The Butterflies

T HE WINGS of a butterfly seem so delicate that it is hard to imagine this fragile insect traveling much farther than from flower to flower. But one beautiful butterfly—the monarch butterfly—is stronger than it looks. For it will travel on its small wings a thousand miles or more. And on its way put on a wonderful show.

Monarch butterflies live in the northern United States and lower parts of Canada. In the summer, they drink from flowers and enjoy the sun.

But when fall comes, and a cooler wind chills their butterfly wings, the monarchs know they must search out a warmer home. They cannot survive the snow and ice of winter. There is only one place to fly now: *south*.

In the east and in the west, the monarchs come together in small groups. Then the small groups join to form one large group. And the glorious monarch migration begins.

On the West Coast, the butterflies will head for California or Mexico. On the East Coast, they will fly to sunny Florida.

Imagine a blue sky covered with beautiful monarch butterflies! What a spectacle! Sometimes there are *millions* of butterflies

flying together, and many towns wait anxiously for them and throw great celebrations when they pass. It is very exciting!

By the end of October, all of the monarchs have flown south. But the show isn't quite over, for in California, the monarchs are about to make "butterfly trees."

The monarchs will settle themselves thickly over the limbs of the great California evergreen trees—thousands of butterflies to

a tree—and the forests will be transformed. What a wondrous sight! Here on the tall trees, the beautiful monarchs will hibernate through the winter months, safely away from the freezing snow and ice of their northern homes.

If some days are warm and sunny, the monarchs may wake and fly a bit. But mostly they will sleep on the great green trees until spring. Then they will rise up and fly north again.

But this time, these beautiful monarchs will not finish their long journey. Instead, on their way north, the male and female butterflies will mate, then die. Their eggs, which have been laid on milkweed plants, will soon hatch into caterpillars, and the caterpillars will become new butterflies. And these children will finish the journey their parents began.

To hungry birds, small butterflies can be a very tempting treat. These new monarchs might all be eaten up before they reach the north if not for a great trick: Birds are made sick by milkweed, and these new butterflies are *full* of the milkweed they fed on as caterpillars. No birds will be having these butterflies for dinner!

So the young butterflies will travel on. Though it is still a mystery how they travel in the right direction, it is thought that perhaps they use the sun, moon, and stars to guide them. They do find the very same fields their parents summered in. And as they gently light among all the flowers of the fields, one of the most beautiful migrations in the world is complete.

The Caribou

MIGRATING ANIMALS sometimes face many dangers as they travel, and this is especially true for the majestic antlered caribou. These animals spend their summers on the tundra near the cold Arctic circle. The weather is mild in summer, the food good and plentiful on the green pastures. However, the caribou cannot stay here long, for they will not survive an Arctic winter. But even migration will not save all of them.

While they summer on the tundra, the caribou spend their time alone or in twos or threes. Their days are calm and lazy and the only real problem they face are flies, which irritate and keep the caribou always moving.

But this peaceful time cannot last. In winter, terrible storms blow across the tundra, making deep layers of ice. The caribou

cannot scrape through the thick ice to reach the food they need. If they winter on the tundra, they will surely die of starvation.

There is only one choice for them: to travel.

As soon as the caribou sense that winter is approaching, they will seek one another out for the long journey south. Two caribou will find each other. These will find ten more. Ten will find fifty. And in time, as many as 100,000 caribou will be together, running toward southern forests.

A migrating herd is an incredible sight. One herd of caribou can be nearly 200 miles long! It can take the herd weeks and weeks just to pass by the same little tree. And the noise of all those hooves! It is both frightening and thrilling.

This is not an easy time for the caribou. The way to the forests is full of risk. There are raging rivers to cross; some caribou will drown. Lakes may be only partly frozen; some caribou will fall through the ice. And wolves will follow the herd day and night.

But on the herd will go, nearly 600 miles across the hard landscape. How do the caribou know how to find the forests?

This remains a mystery. Like other migrating animals, they may sense the earth's magnetic field. Or perhaps the wind tells them, or the shape of the land.

But the herd never loses its way, and finally the caribou are within the forests they know so well. This is where they will spend winter, pawing away the softer snow to reach the vegetation below.

The caribou will not stay in the forests beyond winter, though. For in spring, their calves are going to be born. And a forest full of wolves is no place for new babies!

So the herd forms again, pregnant females in front, males and younger caribou behind. And now running north, they will leave the wolves and nearly all other living creatures behind as they travel to a place where few can survive: the North Pole.

This is a deadly cold, barren land. Even the hungry wolves will not follow the caribou here. But the caribou are made for such a place, and here they do survive, and their calves as well. As spring passes, the babies will have a chance to safely grow and become strong before the herd moves again.

Now the caribou migration is nearly over. The calves are born, spring is ending, summer is near, and the time has come for the caribou to circle back to their beginnings, to the sweet grassy tundra the herd left so many months ago.

The caribou spread across the tundra, the summer sun on their backs, and they split up again into ones, twos, threes. They relax and eat all that a caribou stomach can hold. It is a good time for them.

But in chilly September, each caribou will lift its head and know that things are about to change. One will go searching for another, until soon the thunder of thousands of hooves will signal the beginning of another great, and dangerous, caribou migration.

The Terns

O F A L L migrations, probably the journey of birds is best known to people. Each fall, traveling south, thousands of birds fly over towns and countrysides, and nearly everyone notices.

But incredible as it may seem, there was a time when people did not know that some birds migrate.

Hundreds of years ago, when certain birds disappeared in the winter, some people thought the birds had simply gone inside holes somewhere to sleep until spring.

Others thought the missing birds had actually *changed* into *different* birds for the winter.

But there were some who believed that the birds had traveled far away in winter, and that those same birds would return again in spring. These people were right.

But they would probably never have believed the story of the
little Arctic tern. For of all the birds that migrate, none breaks
the records like this one. It flies farther than any other bird,
and, in fact, covers more migrating miles than any other
creature on the earth. Because every year, this small bird flies
all the way from the North Pole to the South Pole and back

again: *25,000 miles*! It is an astonishing accomplishment. And to do it, the tern must live most of its life always in the air.

The Arctic tern spends its summers near the North Pole. Here the females and males mate, nesting near small streams. When their chicks hatch, the tern parents fish all day long to feed themselves and their babies. They have to

eat as much as they can, for soon they are going to fly 12,000 miles *nonstop*.

In the fall, the little terns set out, flying south. Behind them, the winter winds will soon be howling and the Arctic snow piling up many feet high. It is good these tiny birds have escaped!

They are amazingly strong. They fly over dark forests, tropical islands, endless oceans, and they rarely land. They dip into waters to fish and eat in the air.

How can they endure eight months of flying? And how do they know which way to go? As with other migrating creatures, there are many theories about how birds navigate, but no one really knows for sure.

The small terns will fly and fly through winter, through spring, until finally, in summer, they will reach Antarctica near the South Pole. Summer here is still too cold for most animals. But for the terns, it is perfect. Here they will rest.

And will they eat!

Yet fall comes quickly, and the wind is growing colder. In winter, the temperature in Antarctica can be 100 degrees below zero. This is no place for a little bird to stay!

So the terns, fattened, strength regained, will lift up their wings and fly all the way back to the North Pole. It will take them eight months. But they will travel on, to survive, to live. And after a short rest, they will make the whole trip all over again!

Conclusion

ONE of the most wonderful mysteries on this earth is the migration of its creatures. That they understand when to travel and where to go and *how* to get there is one of the planet's marvels.

Tiny birds, great whales, fragile butterflies, persistent eels, humming locusts, and brave caribou: These are all miracles in motion. Travelers on a remarkable road.

To my father, RVD
—LD

THE BLUE SKY PRESS

Text copyright © 2006 by Cynthia Rylant

Illustrations copyright © 2006 by Lambert Davis

All rights reserved.

For information regarding permission, please write to: Permissions

Department, Scholastic Inc., 557 Broadway, New York, New York 10012.

SCHOLASTIC, THE BLUE SKY PRESS, and associated logos are

trademarks and/or registered trademarks of Scholastic Inc.

Library of Congress catalog card number: 2004020762

ISBN 0-590-30717-7

10 9 8 7 6 5 4 3 2 1   06 07 08 09 10

Printed in Mexico   49

First printing, February 2006

Designed by Kathleen Westray